What the Bible Says About the Heart

THE TRANSFORMED HEART

10 Steps for Spiritual Heart Care

How to Recognize an Unhealthy Heart

The Marks of a Transformed Heart

ROSE PUBLISHING

The Meaning of Heart

Have you noticed how much people talk about the *heart*? They urge, "Stop wearing your heart on your sleeve." "Listen to your heart," they say. "Follow your heart," they declare.

This fixation on the heart, is it a modern phenomenon? Not at all. Long before the invention of Valentine's Day, the heart was already a major focus of the Bible. The wise King Solomon urged, "Above all else, guard your heart, for everything you do flows from it" (Proverbs 4:23). Jesus declared, "A good person produces good things from the treasury of a good heart, and an evil person produces evil things from the treasury of an evil heart. What you say flows from what is in your heart" (Luke 6:45 NLT).

The clear testimony of the Bible is that the condition of our hearts determines the direction of our lives. If our hearts are healthy, our lives will be healthy. If our hearts aren't right, nothing else about our lives will be either.

So what exactly is the *heart?* In more than 800 references, the Bible depicts the heart as that immaterial part of our human personality where we feel and think and decide.

Feelings

When you're overcome by powerful waves of grief or euphoria, that's your heart at work. Love, shame, regret, embarrassment, nostalgic memories—all that is felt in the heart. It's in our hearts that we healthily process (or unhealthily bury) hurtful experiences.

The Bible speaks of . . .

- panicked hearts (Joshua 2:11)
- glad or joyful hearts (1 Kings 8:66; Psalm 19:8)
- wounded hearts (Psalm 109:22)
- bitter hearts (Proverbs 14:10)
- broken hearts (Psalm 34:18)

. . . as well as hearts in the grips of many other strong emotions!

In the Old Testament, ***heart*** is the translation of several Hebrew words, the most common being *leb* (לֵב), which can also mean "inner person" or "mind."

In the New Testament, ***heart*** is translated from the Greek word *kardia* (καρδία), from which we get our English word *cardiologist*.

Thoughts

Most people think your *heart* is your "touchy-feely" side. It's that emotional, sentimental, impulsive side of you. Your *mind*, on the other hand, is where you think. It's the rational, scientific, calculating part of your personality.

The Bible describes the heart as …

- discerning (1 Kings 3:9)
- meditative (Psalm 19:14; 77:6)
- plotting or scheming (Proverbs 6:18)
- planning (Proverbs 16:1)
- reflective or remembering (Luke 2:19, 51)

Interestingly, the ancient Hebrews didn't make such a distinction between the heart and the mind. For them, the intellectual and emotional components of life blurred and overlapped. This explains why the biblical writers often use the terms *heart*, *mind*, and *soul* interchangeably.

According to the Bible, then, your *heart* isn't just where you "get the feels"; it's also where you discern and evaluate. It's in your heart that you analyze, ponder, and wrestle with ideas. Forming opinions, attitudes, values, beliefs, and convictions—all that happens in your heart.

Decisions

The Bible describes the heart as where we declare, "I will _________, but I will not _________." You choose with your heart. It sets the direction of your life and then governs your behavior. Intentions, purposes, motivations, determinations—all that is rooted in your heart.

In showing the heart to be . . .

- stubborn (Jeremiah 9:14; Mark 3:5)
- wayward (1 Kings 11:3–4)
- devoted (Deuteronomy 30:10)
- resolute (Acts 11:23)
- believing (Romans 10:10)

. . . it's clear that the Bible sees the heart as that part of our personhood where we choose.

Putting all this together, the biblical word *heart* refers to your inner, immaterial nature. Your heart is your central essence. It's the core of your personality. It's your human spirit, your "you-ness."

Changing Your Heart

Okay, my heart needs changing! Cut to the chase—how can I change it?

Actually, you can't. Remember the words of Jesus: "Apart from me you can do nothing" (John 15:5)? Only *he* has the power to truly transform our hearts. However, we do have a significant role to play in that process.

What's our role? The answer to this question is found in what Jesus said at the beginning of the gospel of Mark: "Repent and believe the good news!" (Mark 1:15). That is our part: to repent and believe.

Repent literally means "to change your mind." God graciously reveals truth to you, prompting you to rethink your life and begin moving in a new and better direction.

Believe means "to rely upon." We stop relying on our own ideas about where and how to find life. Instead, we begin trusting Jesus to show us the way.

We repented and believed when we first began to follow Jesus, and that is also how we walk with him all the days of our lives.

When you get complacent and wander offtrack, repent and believe. As God reveals unhealthy heart habits and attitudes, acknowledge and renounce them.

If "above all else" we are

- watching over our hearts,
- spending time daily with Jesus,
- nourishing our souls with God's Word,
- stopping to reflect on what's true,
- routinely opening our hearts to the work of God's Spirit,
- daily yielding our agendas and wills to the greater purposes of God,

then—and only then—will we see our hearts transformed. At last we'll experience what Jesus promised—real, new, rich life, bubbling up from our hearts and flowing like a river into the lives of others.

John 7:37-38 NLT

"Anyone who is thirsty may come to me! Anyone who believes in me may come and drink! For the Scriptures declare, 'Rivers of living water will flow from his heart.' "

6. Avail yourself of God's great resources for spiritual health and growth.

You've been given:

- the Word of God to show you what's true,
- the Spirit of God to empower you to live as you should,
- the people of God to encourage you and walk beside you through life,
- the mission of God to give your life purpose and direction.

7. Accept that the process is slow.

Occasionally the process of spiritual healing and growth is rapid, but most of the time it is quite slow. God is not in a hurry. Weeds can spring up overnight, but valuable and beautiful things—like diamonds and oak trees—take much longer to produce.

8. Adjust to the reality that heart health is a lifestyle.

If only we could read a few pages like these here and declare, "Done! Our hearts are now healthy!" It doesn't work that way. We'll never be done watching over our hearts this side of heaven. Remember Solomon—the guy who championed the importance of guarding our hearts? In the end, even his heart was led astray to worship false gods and do evil (see Proverbs 4:23; 1 Kings 11:1–6). We're in this for the long haul, and we can't get complacent.

9. Associate with others who are serious about watching over their hearts.

Ever try to start a new exercise regimen all by yourself? It's tough to keep it going, isn't it? We encounter the same kind of resistance when we pursue spiritual health alone. For that reason, gather some friends. Join a small group. Find an accountability relationship. Together is definitely better.

10. Anticipate both problems and progress.

The enemy of your heart will fiercely oppose your efforts to find and maintain spiritual health (1 Peter 5:8), but the Lover of your heart is greater (1 John 4:4). God will strengthen you, encourage you, and bring wholeness to your heart.

The Marks of a Transformed Heart

The following descriptions show the kind of heart that is possible when we open ourselves to God's transforming presence.

Description	Meaning
A believing heart *Mark 11:23*	To have a heart that relies on the power of God and that fights the temptation to doubt
A broken and contrite heart *Psalm 51:17*	To be spiritually and emotionally crushed by the realization that you have disobeyed a good, loving, and holy God
A changed heart *Romans 2:29 NLT*	To experience a shift in motivation, from external pressure to keep God's law to an internal desire to obey
A committed heart *2 Chronicles 34:31*	To be committed to do whatever God has said, regardless of feelings or circumstances or outcomes
A confident (steadfast) heart *Psalm 57:7*	To be stable and secure in the truth that God rules, reigns, and rescues
A delighted heart *Psalm 37:4*	To be satisfied in God at the core of your being
A desirous heart *Isaiah 28:6*	To long for the things that are near and dear to God's heart
A devoted heart *1 Kings 8:61*	To give your allegiance and affection fully to the one true God and not to false gods or substitute saviors
An enlightened heart *Ephesians 1:18*	To be granted the ability to see and grasp God's eternal truth
An examined heart *Psalm 17:3*	To invite God to search your heart for suspect motives, wrong thoughts, and improper attitudes
A fearless heart *Psalm 27:3, 14*	To have confidence that God is present, protective, and more powerful than anything that comes against you
A forgiving heart *Matthew 18:35*	To pardon—with God's help—the offenses of others from the depths of your being, not just in empty words
A generous heart *Exodus 35:5 NLT*	To be willing and eager to share your resources
A glad heart *Psalm 16:9*	To rejoice deeply in who God is and what he has done
A God-fearing heart *Deuteronomy 5:29*	To be filled with and controlled by a deep reverence for the Lord and a desire to honor him
A God-following heart *1 Kings 14:8*	To be relentless in knowing and doing the will of God
A God-influenced heart *Nehemiah 2:12*	To be wooed or nudged by God to respond to his call

Description	Meaning
A God-obsessed heart *1 Samuel 13:14*	To be one "after [the Lord's] own heart," meaning to love God and his purposes above all else
A good heart *Matthew 12:35*	To have a heart that has been touched and transformed by God so that you are able to please God and bless others
A guarded heart *Proverbs 4:23*	To carefully monitor the condition of your own heart
A happy heart *Proverbs 15:13*	To be joyful, merry, or glad
An honest heart *Luke 8:15 NLT*	To be noble or honorable (receptive) when presented with God's truth
A humble heart *Matthew 11:29*	To refuse to exalt yourself; to be unpretentious
A heart indwelt by Christ *Ephesians 3:17*	To treat Christ as your soul's guest of honor as he lives in you and you live for him
A heart indwelt by the Holy Spirit *2 Corinthians 1:22*	To rest secure in the knowledge that the Holy Spirit in your heart is a guarantee that God will do everything he has promised you
A heart of integrity *Genesis 20:5*	To be completely upright in all, not just some, areas of life
A heart of love and faithfulness *Proverbs 3:3*	To allow the loyal love of God to so fill and change your soul that God's kindness and faithfulness flows out of you
A loving heart *Deuteronomy 6:5*	To have deep affection for and undying devotion to another —demonstrated by active concern and/or service
A new heart *Ezekiel 36:26*	To experience God's supernatural replacement of your "old heart" that was unresponsive to the things of God with a "new heart" that is eager and able to love and serve him
An obedient heart *Romans 6:17*	To have a heart that says "not my will, but your will be done"
An "on-course" heart *Proverbs 23:19*	To set your heart (and, thus, your life) on God's path
A peaceful heart *John 14:27*	To rest in the promises of Jesus so that you are set free from the fear of worldly difficulties
A praying heart *Psalm 119:145*	To cry desperately to God from the depths of your being
A prepared heart *Job 11:13*	To be established or made ready for the work God wants to do in and through you

A Healthy Heart Checklist: 10 Action Steps

***Entropy* is the** scientific law that describes the way physical things naturally decline into a state of disorder. We see this law at work in an old, abandoned house: the sagging roof, the peeling paint, the rotting siding. Everything in our fallen world requires regular maintenance—including our hearts. If we don't watch over them regularly, a kind of spiritual entropy will take over. Here is a checklist for regular maintenance to have a spiritually healthy heart:

1. Ask (and answer) some tough questions.

- Do I believe the Bible's teaching about my heart?
- Does the kind of life I live really depend on the kind of heart I have?
- What will happen if I don't give attention to my heart?

2. Assess the state of your heart.

Look at the "heart charts" in these pages. Prayerfully and carefully ponder what the Bible says about healthy (and not-so-healthy) hearts. Listen to what flows out of your mouth. Make an honest inventory of your current behaviors and habits, resisting the urge to rationalize, minimize, or justify.

3. Acknowledge what you find.

If a close examination of your heart/life reveals some ugly truths, don't live in denial. We can never get healthy until we first admit we are sick (Mark 2:17). Also, don't despair of any junk you find in your life. God has seen it all—many, many times before. The good news is that he is all-powerful and perfectly gracious. He is the great healer of hearts. You are utterly safe within his care.

4. Agree to God's treatment plan.

Realize that God doesn't prescribe superficial solutions. He is going to probe your soul and do surgery on your heart. Rather than simplistic answers—"Just stay off social media for a while" or "Cancel your cable service"—he is going to ask harder questions like: "How about we explore what is underneath all those angry online rants?" or "Why is your heart so attached to sexually explicit videos? What makes you think you can find life there?"

5. Acquire new "heart healthy" habits.

In the same way that physical exercise fosters physical health, spiritual exercise promotes spiritual health. Humbly engage in spiritual disciplines such as prayer, Bible reading, confession, worship, generosity, and telling others about your faith. These can bring healing and strength to your heart.

Spiritual Heart Care

One of the best-known biblical statements about the heart is from wise King Solomon: "Above all else, guard your heart, for everything you do flows from it" (Proverbs 4:23). Here, in one succinct proverb, is a brilliant, short course in spiritual heart care.

What does heart care involve?

Solomon urged us to **guard** our hearts. This word *guard* is often used in prison contexts or in passages describing the threat of invasion. It means "to confine; take custody of; to post guards; to watch over carefully; to be on high alert" (Genesis 40:3; 42:17; Nehemiah 4:16; 7:3; Numbers 15:34; Jeremiah 51:12). In other words, this is different from being guarded and aloof around people. *Guard* means to keep an eye on your heart, monitor it, watch it like a hawk.

What difference does heart care make?

"**Everything** you do flows from [your heart]." Or as one translation renders this: "Your heart . . . is the wellspring of life" (WEB). The original Hebrew here is fascinating; the basic meaning is to go out, come out, or go forth—like a spring bubbling up from the earth. Solomon meant that whatever is on the inside of us is going to exit to the outside. In short, our hearts are the source or starting point of our lives. We all know what happens when a spring is tainted at its source. The water downstream is undrinkable and unhealthy. Are you starting to get the picture? Your heart is *everything!*

How much of a priority should we make heart care?

"**Above all else,**" Solomon said. Spiritual heart care is not a nice, optional thing to do *if* we happen to think about it or *if* we manage to find a little extra time. No, we must make time for this vital practice. Watching over our hearts should be our top priority.

In short, whatever is in your heart will eventually come to the surface of your life. That can either be a good thing: love for God, compassion for people, thankfulness for God's grace, etc. Or it can be greed, lust, anger, bitterness, a love of money, insecurity, and lots of other unlovely qualities.

Description	Meaning
A pure heart *Matthew 5:8*	To be morally clean and free from guilt
A rejoicing heart *Zephaniah 3:14*	To celebrate with passion the goodness and blessings of God
A responsive heart *Psalm 27:8*	To yield to, rather than resist, God's invitations
A searching heart *Deuteronomy 4:29*	To be in earnest, ongoing pursuit of God
A serving heart *Deuteronomy 10:12*	To expend energy or labor on behalf of another; to give worship and devotion to God
A sincere heart *Acts 2:46*	To be genuine, single-minded in your purpose to be devoted in service to God
A stirred-up heart *2 Chronicles 36:22 NLT*	To be sensitive and responsive to the promptings of God and the needs of others
A teachable heart *Proverbs 4:4*	To humbly accept instruction, cling to it, and obey it
A tested heart *Proverbs 17:3*	To have a heart that has undergone trials and has proven to be pure
A thankful heart *Psalm 9:1*	To be grateful and appreciative for God's many blessings
A true heart *Acts 11:23*	To be loyal and devoted; to cling fiercely and faithfully
A trusting heart *Proverbs 3:5*	To have faith that God's heart and will are good, with the result that you entrust your future and well-being to him
An undivided heart *Psalm 86:11*	To be wholehearted in your commitment to God
A unified heart *Acts 4:32*	To experience unity with other believers around a shared belief in the gospel of Jesus
A wise heart *Psalm 90:12*	To be guided skillfully through life by God's truth
A Word-filled heart *Psalm 40:8*	To "take God's Word to heart," meaning, to internalize it through repeated reading and Scripture memory so that it is available to guide you in various life situations
A yielded heart *Joshua 24:23*	To be surrendered to the authority of the Lord

Monitoring Your Heart

When you suspect something is wrong with your "ticker," you go see your doctor. But what about when there is something wrong with your *spiritual* heart? Acts 1:24 describes God as the *kardiognostes*—the "knower of hearts." He is able to see and search the hidden depths of our hearts (1 Samuel 16:7; Luke 16:15; Romans 8:27; 1 Thessalonians 2:4). Is it time for you to make an appointment with the divine cardiologist?

Condition	Question to Ask
A backsliding heart *Proverbs 14:14* NASB	Am I turning my back on or moving away from biblical truths I once believed?
A bitter heart *Ephesians 4:31*	Am I harboring resentment or a grudge against anyone?
A crooked heart *Proverbs 17:20*	In my thinking, speaking, and choosing, am I deviating from the life to which God calls his people?
A cunning heart *Psalm 64:6*	Am I dreaming or scheming about actions that are dishonoring to God or hurtful to others?
A deceitful heart *Jeremiah 17:9*	Am I guilty of dishonesty or shading the truth in my interactions with God or others?
A divided heart *2 Kings 10:31*	Am I wholly devoted to the Lord or am I withholding certain areas of my life from him?
A foolish heart *Proverbs 22:15*	Am I living in a way that godly people would say is wise?
A grieving heart *Proverbs 15:13; Lamentations 2:11*	In grieving a loss or reeling from a devastating trial, am I turning to the one who heals the brokenhearted (Psalm 147:3)?
A hard heart *Ephesians 4:18*	Am I resistant to God's word or will?
A lusting heart *Matthew 5:28; Romans 1:24*	Am I giving in to the impure desires that ruled my life before I began following Christ?
A numb heart *Acts 2:37* NLT	Do I feel conviction ("pierced to the heart") when I do something sinful, or is my heart numb?
A proud heart *Psalm 131:1; Proverbs 21:4*	Am I arrogant—thinking chiefly of *my* desires, pushing for *my* ideas, promoting *my* agenda?
A troubled heart *John 14:1; Job 30:27* NLT	Am I so stirred up, agitated, and upset that I have a hard time sleeping or focusing?
A vacillating heart *1 Kings 18:21; James 1:8*	Am I wavering in my spiritual life—trying to ride the proverbial fence between spiritual and fleshly things?

OUR EXTERNAL LIFE

Words: What we say

Actions: What we do

OUR INTERNAL LIFE

What trips us up:

- Unprocessed hurts
- Unconscious and/or unhealthy attitudes
- Paralyzing fears
- Powerful regrets

What drives us:

- Beliefs (both right and wrong)
- Dreams, goals, ambitions (both noble and selfish)
- Pure and impure motives
- Holy and unholy desires
- Whatever we truly love and worship

What we try to hide:

- Failures and flaws
- Secret sins
- Whatever makes us feel ashamed

Spiritual heart care is vital.

The kind of life we live depends on the kind of heart we have.

Addressing Spiritual Heart Issues

Perhaps in looking at the "heart charts" in these pages—and in surveying your life—you're thinking, *I have some spiritual issues that need prompt attention. What now?*

Sometimes when people get to this place, they conclude that they just need to *know* more about God and *do* more for God and then their hearts will be fixed. While this thinking isn't incorrect, it is incomplete. Engaging in good Bible studies, spiritual discussions, and ministry efforts doesn't automatically mean that we are addressing the harder-to-see issues lurking deep in our souls.

Remember the scribes and Pharisees in the Bible? Nobody knew God's Word better or could discuss it more eloquently than they. Certainly nobody worked more feverishly to obey it. When it came to *knowing* and *doing*, these religious experts were at the head of the class! And yet Jesus said this about them: "These people honor me with their lips, but their hearts are far from me" (Mark 7:6). They had reduced the spiritual life to possessing the "right" beliefs and practicing the "right" behaviors.

Our hearts can't be transformed by focusing solely on externals. That's like treating a heart attack with a Band-Aid®! God's desire is to transform us from the inside out. That means letting him address all the unhealthy stuff that is buried deep in our hearts.

Asking Jesus into Your Heart

In many churches, it's common to hear people talk about "asking Jesus into your heart." This exact phrase is not found in Scripture, but it likely originated from verses such as Ephesians 3:17—"that Christ may dwell in your hearts through faith"—and Revelation 3:20, where Jesus says to believers, "Here I am! I stand at the door and knock. If anyone hears my voice and opens the door, I will come in and eat with that person, and they with me."

Reflection Questions

1. **What surprises you** most about the Bible's teaching on the heart?

2. **Augustine observed that** people give their hearts to whatever they think will make them happy (if not to God, then to something else). In a prayer to God he concluded, "Our hearts are restless, until they can find rest in you." Do you agree with Augustine's diagnosis? Why or why not?

3. **What five adjectives** best describe your current heart condition?

4. **Who knows best** how you're really doing—in the depths of your soul?

5. **If you were** a spiritual counselor, and *you* came to *you* for help, what counsel would you give yourself?

6. **What is your** specific plan for cultivating a healthier heart?

HENDRICKSON PUBLISHERS
ROSE PUBLISHING
www.hendricksonrose.com

Author: Len Woods

Printed in the USA. 030319SCG

RELIGION/Biblical Studies/General

ISBN 978-162862-334-5

9 781628 623345

Product Code 4100X *The Transformed Heart* pamphlet
Retailers: Package of 5 pamphlets = Stock #4101X (ISBN-13: 9781628623376)